WISDOM
of
WOLVES

Art Director: Brian MacMullen
Designer: Neil Dvorak
Editor: Rachael Lanicci
Photo Researcher: Benjamin DeWalt

Metro Books
122 Fifth Avenue
New York, NY 10011

ISBN-13: 978-1-4351-0536-2
ISBN-10: 1-4351-0536-2

Printed and bound in China

1 . 3 5 7 9 10 8 6 4 2

WISDOM
— of —
WOLVES

Compiled by
Rachael Lanicci

METRO BOOKS
NEW YORK

"May the stars
carry your
sadness away,
May the flowers
fill your heart
with **beauty**,
May hope
forever
wipe away
your tears . . .

. . . And, **above all**,
may silence make you **strong**."

–*Chief Dan George*

"Follow **humbly** wherever and to whatever abyss **Nature** leads, or you shall **learn** nothing."

–*Thomas Henry Huxley*

"You can't do anything about the **length** of your life, but you can **do something** about its **width** and **depth.**"

–*Shira Tehrani*

"Accept **challenges**, so that you may feel the exhilaration of **victory**."

–*George S. Patton*

"We are like tea bags—
we don't know our
own **strength** until
we're in **hot water**."

–*Sister Busche*

"The journey of a
thousand miles must
begin with a
single step."

–*Lao Tzu*

"Your **worth** consists in what you **are** and not in what you **have**."

–*Thomas Edison*

"To keep our faces toward change and behave like **free** spirits in the presence of fate is strength **undefeatable**."

–*Helen Keller*

"We must **learn** to live together as **brothers** or **perish** together as **fools**."

–Martin Luther King Jr.

"World peace, like community peace, does **not require** that each man love his neighbor; it requires only that they live with **mutual tolerance**, submitting their disputes to a **just** and **peaceful settlement**."

–*John F. Kennedy*

"A **moment's** insight
is sometimes worth
a life's experience."

–Oliver Wendall Holmes

"Happiness is not a matter of events,

it depends upon the tides of the mind.

–Alice Meynell

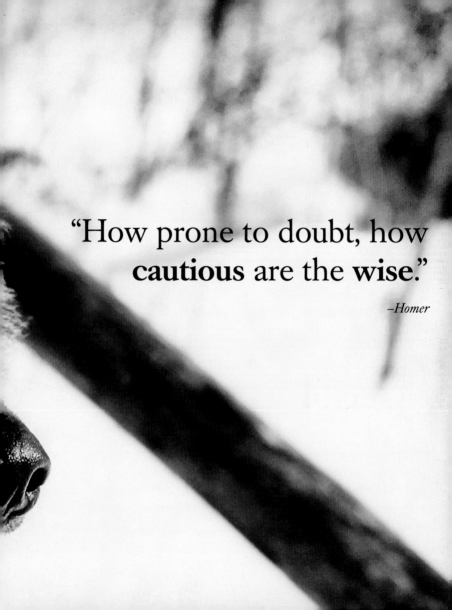

"How prone to doubt, how **cautious** are the **wise**."

–*Homer*

"Fortify yourself
with **contentment**,
for this is
an **impregnable** fortress."

–Epictetus

"Nothing should be **prized** more highly than the **value** of each day."

–Johann Wolfgang van Goethe

"A **loving** heart
is the
truest wisdom."

–*Charles Dickens*

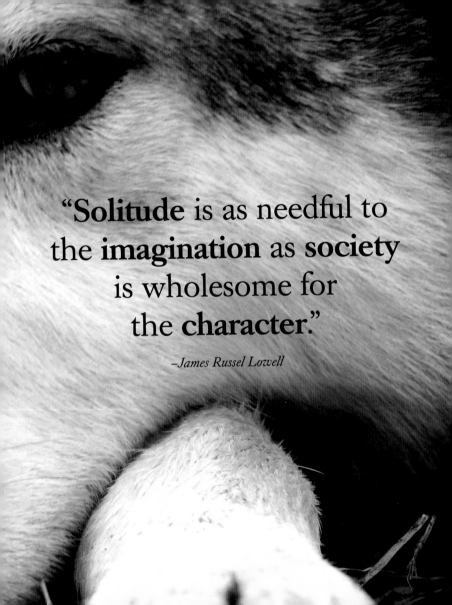

"**Solitude** is as needful to the **imagination** as **society** is wholesome for the **character**."

–*James Russel Lowell*

"Kind words can be easy to speak but their **echoes** are truly **e n d l e s s**."

–Mother Teresa

"All misfortune
is but a
stepping stone
to fortune."

–*Henry David Thoreau*

"It is good to **rub** and **polish** our brains against that of others."

–*Michel de Montaigne*

"Time in its aging course
teaches all things."

–Aeschylus

"Where there is **love**, there is no darkness."

–Burundi proverb

"The bird that would **soar above** the level plain of tradition and prejudice must have **strong** wings."

–Kate Chopin

"We are **here** on Earth to fart around. Don't let **anybody** tell you any different."

–Kurt Vonnegut

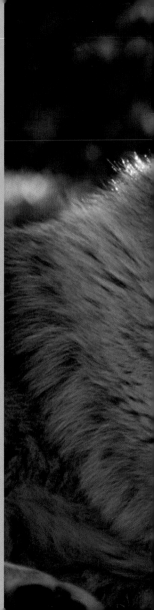

"Genius might be the **ability** to **say** a **profound** thing in a **simple** way."

–*Charles Bukowski*

"Freedom lies in being bold."

–Robert Frost

"Our greatest fear is not that we are inadequate, but that we are **powerful** beyond measure."

–*Nelson Mandela*

"**Big** things are expected of us, and nothing big ever came of being small."

–*William Jefferson Clinton*

"**No one** can make you feel inferior without your **consent**."

–*Eleanor Roosevelt*

"The secret to flying

is to throw yourself at the
ground and **miss**."

–Douglas Adams

"Nothing is so strong as **gentleness**, and nothing is so gentle as **true strength**."

–*Ralph Sockman*

"Who is the happier man, he who has **braved** the storm of life and lived, or he who has stayed securely on shore and merely **existed**?"

–*Hunter S. Thompson*

"An **idea**,
like a ghost, must be
spoken to
a little before
it will
explain itself."

–Charles Dickens

"You should **examine** yourself daily. If you find faults, you should **correct** them. When you find none, you should **try** even harder."

–*Wang Xizhi*

"Of course it's trivial, but then **most** things are."

–*John Malkovich*

"The less men **think,**
the more they **talk.**"

–*Charles de Montesquieu*

"We build **too many walls** and not enough **bridges.**"

–Isaac Newton

"**Anyone** can be heroic
from time to time,
but a **gentleman**
is something
you have to be
all the time."

–Luigi Pirandello

"The **only** Zen
you can find
on the **tops**
of mountains
is the Zen you
bring up there."

–*Robert M. Pirsig*

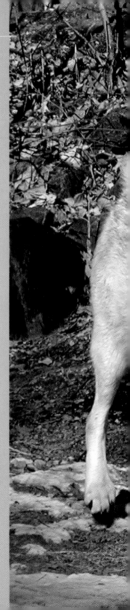

"Be **kind**,
for **everyone**
you meet
is fighting a
hard battle."

–*Plato*

"The **mind** is not
a vessel to be filled
but a **fire** to be **kindled**."

–*Plutarch*

"To **know** oneself is to study oneself in **action** with another person."

–*Bruce Lee*

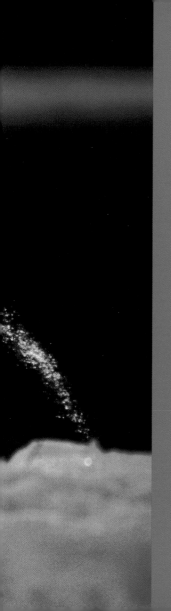

"**Life** is not a matter of holding **good** cards, but sometimes, playing a poor hand **well**."

–*Jack London*

"Of all the things you **wear**, your expression is the most **important**."

–*Janet Lane*

"How much do you **engage** yourself in what's truly **real and important** in life? That's the individual question."

–Ted Danson

"There is no such thing
in **anyone's** life
as an unimportant day."

–Alexander Woollcott

"There are only two mistakes one can make along the road to **truth**; *not* **going all the way,** and *not* **starting.**"

–*Buddha*

"The future belongs
to those who **believe**
in the **beauty**
of their **dreams.**"

–Eleanor Roosevelt

"The pleasantest things in the world are **pleasant thoughts**: and the great art of life is to have as **many** of them as possible."

–*Montaigne*

"Time spent **laughing** is time spent with the gods."

–Japanese proverb

"There can be **hope** only
for a society which acts as
one big family,
not as many separate ones."

–*Anwar Sadat*

"The more you are
motivated by **love**,
the more **fearless and free**
your actions will be."

–*Dalai Lama*

"The proper function of man is **to live**, not to exist."

–*Jack London*

"I do not know of any **poetry** to quote

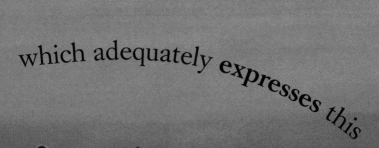

which adequately expresses this

yearning for the wild".

–Henry David Thoreau

"Little progress
can be made by
merely attempting
to repress what is evil.
Our **great hope** lies
in developing
what is good."

–*Calvin Coolidge*

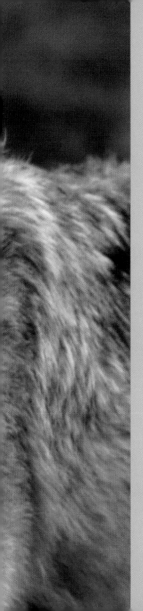

"Be **glad** of life,
because it **gives
you** the chance
to love and
to work
and to play
and to **look up
at the stars.**"

–*Henry Van Dyke*

"**Seek** the wisdom of the ages, but **look** at the world through the eyes of a **child**."

–*Ron Wild*

PICTURE CREDITS